World History & Cultures

Juan Ponce de León

Explorer of the Americas

by
Wendy Frey

Don Johnston Incorporated
Volo, Illinois

Edited by:

John Bergez
Start-to-Finish Core Content Series Editor, Pacifica, California

Gail Portnuff Venable, MS, CCC-SLP
Speech/Language Pathologist, San Francisco, California

Dorothy Tyack, MA
Learning Disabilities Specialist, San Francisco, California

Jerry Stemach, MS, CCC-SLP
Speech/Language Pathologist, Director of Content Development, Sonoma County, California

Graphics and Illustrations:

Photographs and illustrations are all created professionally and modified to provide the best possible support for the intended reader.
Pages 11, 28: © 2006 JupiterImages Corporation
Pages 13, 38, and back cover: Courtesy of Eon Images
Page 18: Courtesy of the Library of Congress, Print and Photograph Division [LC-USZC2-1687]
Page 25: © Werner Forman/CORBIS
Page 30: Courtesy of the NOAA
Page 42: Courtesy of the Library of Congress, Print and Photograph Division [LC-USZ62-79801]
Page 46 and front cover: Courtesy of the Library of Congress, Print and Photograph Division [LC-USZ62-3106]
Page 49: Drawing by Merald Clark, courtesy Florida Museum of Natural History
Page 51: © Isa Burger/Istockphoto.com
All other photos not credited here or with the photo are © Don Johnston Incorporated and its licensors.

Narration:

Professional actors and actresses read the text to build excitement and to model research-based elements of fluency: intonation, stress, prosody, phrase groupings and rate. The rate has been set to maximize comprehension for the reader.

Published by:

Don Johnston Incorporated
26799 West Commerce Drive
Volo, IL 60073

800.999.4660 USA Canada
800.889.5242 Technical Support
www.donjohnston.com

International Standard Book Number
ISBN 978-1-4105-0906-2

Contents

Getting Started 4

Article 1
From Spain to the Americas 8

Article 2
Life in the Americas 20

Article 3
Discovering a Continent 33

Article 4
The Second Voyage to Florida 44

Glossary 56

About the Author 57

About the Narrator 58

A Note to the Teacher 59

Getting Started

At the beginning of the 1500s, people who lived in Europe did not know much about the **Americas**. (The Americas include North America, South America, and the islands in the Caribbean Sea.) After Christopher Columbus sailed to the Caribbean Sea in 1492, Europeans knew that there was some land between Europe and Asia. But they pictured this land as being made up of islands. They did not know about the huge continents of North and South America.

All kinds of stories were told about the islands that the explorers from Europe were discovering. One story was about the water from a magic spring or fountain.

The story said that the water from this
fountain could make old people young again,
so it was called the Fountain of Youth.

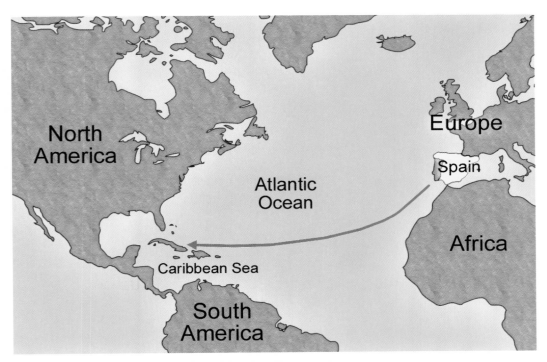

In 1492, Columbus sailed from Spain
to the Caribbean Sea.

King Ferdinand of Spain heard the stories about the Fountain of Youth, and in 1513, he sent Juan Ponce de León to look for it. Ponce de León was a soldier and an explorer. In the 1490s, he had sailed with Christopher Columbus on Columbus's second voyage to the Americas.

Ponce de León

Ponce de León never did find the Fountain of Youth, but he did become one of Spain's most important explorers. In this book, you'll travel with Ponce de León to the Americas and find out how his discoveries changed the world.

Article 1

From Spain to the Americas

Questions this article will answer:

- **How did Ponce de León learn to be a soldier?**

- **When Ponce de León became a soldier for Spain, who did he fight against?**

- **Why did Ponce de León go to the Americas in 1493?**

Juan Ponce de León woke up to the rolling of the ship, just as he had every day for a month. The year was 1493. Ponce de León was on his way to the Americas from Spain. He was traveling with Columbus on Columbus's second voyage.

Ponce de León had never been to sea. He had been excited about starting out on the adventure, but it was turning out to be an awful trip. The ship was crowded. No one had taken a bath since the ship sailed, and everyone smelled bad. The bread was moldy. There were rats and cockroaches everywhere. And most of the men on the ship were seasick.

Ponce de León crossed the ocean
on a ship like this one.

Suddenly, Ponce de León heard a shout.
The lookout was calling out *Tierra!* (Land!).
Ponce de León rushed onto the deck. The
sun was just coming up. There, right in front
of him, was a beautiful, green island. It was
his first look at the Americas.

That day was the beginning of Ponce de León's adventures in the Americas. In this article, you will learn how Ponce de León became an explorer, and why he came to the Americas.

When Ponce de León got his first look at the Americas, he might have seen something like this.

Learning to Be a Soldier

Ponce de León was born in about 1474 in Spain. When he was a boy, his parents sent him to the home of a **knight** named Don Pedro. (*Don* means "Sir" in Spanish.) Knights were soldiers who fought on horseback for the king. Ponce de León learned to be a soldier by working for Don Pedro.

Ponce de León did many things for Don Pedro. He polished his armor and his sword. He helped take care of his horse. He brought him his meals. And he helped Don Pedro to put on his armor before battles.

He also learned the skills that soldiers needed to know. He learned to ride horseback and to fight with a sword. As he grew up, Ponce de León became a good soldier.

A Spanish knight

Fighting the Moors

When Ponce de León was about 18, he fought in a war against the Moors. The Moors were Muslims who lived in northern Africa and southern Spain.

King Ferdinand and Queen Isabella had two reasons for starting a war to drive the Moors out of Spain. Their first reason was that the Moors were Muslim, and Ferdinand and Isabella wanted Christianity to be the only religion in Spain. The second reason was that the Moors were rulers of part of Spain, and Ferdinand and Isabella wanted to rule all of Spain themselves.

King Ferdinand and Queen Isabella

In 1491, Ferdinand and Isabella sent their army to Granada, the Moors' capital city. There was a great battle. Men in metal suits of armor fought each other face-to-face, and tried to chop each other to death with iron swords. Ponce de León took part in that bloody battle.

The Moors fought hard, but the Spanish army was much larger. By the beginning of 1492, the Spanish forced the Moors to surrender.

The Moors in Granada had to surrender to King Ferdinand and Queen Isabella.

Ponce de León was happy about the victory over the Moors. But he had a problem. With the war over, there was less work for soldiers.

Sailing with Columbus

Soon after the war ended, Ponce de León heard some exciting news. He heard that the great explorer Christopher Columbus was setting sail for the Americas again.

On his first voyage in 1492, Columbus had sailed west across the Atlantic Ocean. He was hoping to reach China. Columbus did not know that the Americas were in his path. On the voyage, he discovered several islands just south of North America.

Columbus landing on an island in the Americas in 1492

Now, Ferdinand and Isabella were sending Columbus back to the islands he had discovered. This time, they wanted him to bring back gold. He would take 17 ships and 1200 men with him. Columbus was looking for soldiers to go with him. Ponce de León signed up for the voyage right away.

On September 25, 1493, Ponce de León set sail for the Americas with Christopher Columbus. As you read at the beginning of this article, it turned out to be a hard trip. But for Ponce de León, the trip was worth it. Now he could look forward to new adventures and beautiful new lands to explore.

Summary

In this article, you read about the early life of Ponce de León. He learned to be a soldier by serving a knight. When he was about 18, he took part in a great battle against the Moors. After the war ended, there was less work for soldiers in Spain, so Ponce de León joined the second voyage of Christopher Columbus and sailed to the Americas.

Article 2

Life in the Americas

Questions this article will answer:

- **How did the Spanish treat the native people who lived in the Americas?**

- **What work did Ponce de León do on the island of Hispaniola?**

- **What was his job on the island of Puerto Rico?**

When Ponce de León came to the islands of the Americas, he thought they were the most beautiful places he had ever seen. The islands were green, with many trees and mountains. The air was warm and sweet. But the Spanish did not stop to do much exploring. Christopher Columbus was eager to get back to an island that he had discovered on his first voyage. Columbus called the island Hispaniola. He had left 40 men there to start a **settlement** (a new place where people have come to live).

As the ships approached Hispaniola, Ponce de León expected to see Spanish buildings. And he expected to see Spanish men waiting to greet them. But there were no buildings, and there were no Spanish men.

When Columbus and his men went on shore, they discovered that the people on the island had killed the Spanish and burned the Spanish fort.

People fighting against the Spanish on Hispaniola

In this article, you will learn about the problems between the Spanish and the native people (the people who were living in the Americas). You will also learn what happened to Ponce de León during the time that he lived on two of the islands of the Americas.

How the Spanish Treated the Native People

The islands where Ponce de León sailed with Christopher Columbus are called the Caribbean Islands. These islands are just south and east of Florida.

The Caribbean Islands are in the Caribbean Sea. Three of these islands are called Cuba, Hispaniola, and Puerto Rico.

There were native people living in the Caribbean Islands long before the Spanish came. The people who lived on Hispaniola were called the Taino.

The Taino were a peaceful people. They lived in villages of one or two thousand people. They built round houses out of wooden poles, branches, grass, and vines. They farmed the land, and they fished in long narrow boats called canoes. They made weapons out of wood, and they used these weapons for hunting. They also made fine carvings.

A carving that was made by the Taino

When the Spanish had come to the islands the first time, they had treated the Taino very badly. The men that Columbus had left behind on Hispaniola had demanded gold from the Taino. They had also tried to force the Taino to work for them. The Taino did not like being treated in this way. They fought back and killed the Spanish.

On this second visit to the island, Columbus started another settlement. Soon, more Spanish came and the settlement grew larger.

The Spanish did not treat the native islanders any better the second time they came. They forced the Taino to work in gold mines, digging gold out of the earth. They killed all the Taino who fought back. They sent some Taino people back to Spain as slaves. Many other Taino died of diseases that the Spanish brought with them.

The Spanish treated the Taino very badly.

From Soldier to Wealthy Farmer on Hispaniola

Ponce de León was a Spanish soldier, so it was his job to fight the native people of the islands. In 1502, a war started between the Spanish and the Taino on Hispaniola. The Spanish had swords and guns and the Taino had only bows and arrows, so the Spanish defeated them quickly.

The Spanish settlers were grateful to Ponce de León for protecting them. They gave him a **plantation** (a large farm) as a reward.

Ponce de León became a farmer on Hispaniola. He grew sweet potatoes, corn, sugarcane, and bananas.

A banana plantation

Ponce de León also grew cassava. Cassava was a plant that the Taino used in baking bread. Cassava bread was good to eat, and it stayed fresh for a long time.

Ponce de León sold cassava bread to sailors who were returning to Spain. His farm did well, and he became wealthy. He married a woman on Hispaniola, and they began to raise a family.

Ponce de León could have lived the rest of his life on Hispaniola, but he was still looking for adventure. He had heard stories about an island called Puerto Rico, which was about 200 miles east of Hispaniola. In 1506, Ponce de León said goodbye to his family and set sail for Puerto Rico with 5 ships and 200 men.

Governor of Puerto Rico

Puerto Rico was a lot like Hispaniola. It was a beautiful island with mountains, forests, and sandy beaches. It had good **harbors** for Spanish ships. (A harbor is a place where ships can stay and be protected from bad weather.) The Taino people also told Ponce de León that there was gold on the island of Puerto Rico.

A beach in Puerto Rico

When King Ferdinand in Spain heard about the gold on Puerto Rico, he asked Ponce de León to start a Spanish settlement there and send gold back to Spain. And that's just what Ponce de León did. He brought his family from Hispaniola to Puerto Rico and started a settlement there. He also started several gold mines.

King Ferdinand was pleased with the work Ponce de León was doing. In 1509, the king rewarded Ponce de León by making him the governor of Puerto Rico.

Ponce de León was happy on Puerto Rico. But King Ferdinand wanted him to keep exploring the Americas. The king had heard that there were other beautiful islands farther north. And there were those stories about the magic Fountain of Youth that could make old people young again. King Ferdinand wanted Ponce de León to explore the islands and find the magic fountain.

Once again, Ponce de León said goodbye to his family. He was off on another adventure. He did not know it yet, but this one would make him famous.

Summary

In this article, you learned about Ponce de León's life on the Caribbean Islands. The Spanish treated the Taino people on the Caribbean Islands very badly, and the Taino fought back. Ponce de León led the Spanish in the fighting, and the Spanish quickly defeated the Taino. Ponce de León was given a large farm as a reward, and he became a wealthy farmer.

A few years later, Ponce de León went to a new island called Puerto Rico. He started a settlement there and became the governor. Then King Ferdinand sent Ponce de León on a new adventure — to find the Fountain of Youth.

Article 3

Discovering a Continent

Questions this article will answer:

- Why did Ponce de León choose the name Florida for the new land that he discovered?

- What is the Gulf Stream?

- What kind of people did Ponce de León meet in Florida?

In 1513, Ponce de León left Puerto Rico and sailed north to do more exploring for King Ferdinand. No one knows for sure now whether Ponce de León really believed in the Fountain of Youth. He probably did not think it was real. But he did want to go exploring.

Ponce de León took 3 ships and 65 men with him on this voyage. For a time, they sailed past islands that had already been explored by the Spanish. Then they sailed into waters where no ships from Europe had ever been. There were no maps to help the Europeans find their way.

After almost a month at sea, they saw land ahead of them at last. This land seemed to stretch as far as they could see.

Ponce de León thought that they had discovered a very big island. He did not know that he had discovered an entire continent — the continent of North America.

In this article, you will read how Ponce de León explored part of this new continent. You will also learn about another important discovery that he made.

This is the kind of place that Ponce de León might have seen when he landed in North America.

Finding and Naming Florida

No one knows the exact place where Ponce de León first landed on the North American continent. It was probably near the place where the city of St. Augustine is now, in the state of Florida.

The red dot on the map shows where Ponce de León may have landed when he arrived in North America.

The men went on shore and raised the Spanish flag. As Ponce de León looked around him, he tried to think of a good name for this place.

Ponce de León had just celebrated Easter with his men. In Spanish, Easter is called *Pascua Florida*, which means the "feast of the flowers."

37

Easter was a very important day for the Spanish, and Ponce de León was standing in a place with many beautiful flowers. So he decided to name the new place Florida.

Ponce de León's men in Florida

Discovering the Gulf Stream

Next, Ponce de León's three ships sailed south, down the coast of Florida. Before long, Ponce de León saw that something strange was happening. Even though the wind was filling the sails, the ships were not going forward. They were going backwards!

Ponce de León had discovered the Gulf Stream. The Gulf Stream is a warm, fast-moving current of water — almost like a river or stream in the middle of the ocean. The Gulf Stream begins in the Gulf of Mexico and flows north along the east coast of Florida. Then it travels north and east into the Atlantic Ocean.

The Gulf Stream flows north and east into the Atlantic Ocean.

Ponce de León's discovery of the Gulf Stream was as important as his discovery of Florida. Later on, sailors would be able to use the Gulf Stream to help them sail north and get their ships back to Europe faster.

But Ponce de León did not want to go north, so he sailed his ships out of the Gulf Stream and started to go south again. The ships went around the tip of Florida and traveled up its west coast.

Exploring Florida

From time to time, Ponce de León and his men went on shore to explore. The people he met in Florida were fierce fighters. Several times, native people attacked him and his men with bows and arrows, and the Spanish had to go back to their ships.

41

Native people in Florida carrying a bride to her wedding

Soon Ponce de León was ready to
go home. He returned to Puerto Rico in
October 1513. He had been gone almost
eight months. Ponce de León had not found
the Fountain of Youth for the king, but he
had done much more than that. He had
discovered a new land and named it Florida.
And he had discovered the Gulf Stream.

Summary

In this article, you learned how Ponce de León discovered the continent of North America. When he came ashore on North America, he called the new land Florida. Ponce de León also discovered the Gulf Stream. When Ponce de León and his men went on shore to explore Florida, they met native people who were fierce fighters. After several months in Florida, Ponce de León returned to Puerto Rico.

Article 4

The Second Voyage to Florida

Questions this article will answer:

- **How was Ponce de León's second trip to Florida different from his first one?**

- **What happened when the Calusa Indians attacked the Spanish?**

- **How did Ponce de León's discoveries change the world?**

When King Ferdinand heard about Ponce de León's discoveries in the Americas, he was very pleased. He gave Ponce de León many honors. One of the biggest honors was to make him a knight. The explorer's full name was now Don Juan Ponce de León.

Even more important, King Ferdinand sent Ponce de León back to Florida to start a Spanish settlement there. Ponce de León was eager to do as the king asked. It sounded like another adventure.

Ponce de León became a knight and went
back to Florida to start a settlement there.

In this article, you will find out what
happened during Ponce de León's second
voyage to Florida. You will also learn how
his discoveries changed the world.

Return to Florida

In 1521, Ponce de León sailed for Florida again. This was a very different voyage from the first one. The first time, he had only taken soldiers and sailors with him to explore the new land. This time, his two ships were bringing **settlers** (people who go to a new place or country and build homes there). Some of the settlers were farmers and carpenters. The two ships also carried seeds, tools, and farm animals.

After crossing the ocean, the Spanish settlers landed in Florida and unloaded their supplies. Soon they were building houses and planting crops.

For a while, everything went well for the Spanish. But their good luck did not last long. The native people who lived in Florida did not want the Spanish to stay. This was their home, and they were not going to let the Spanish take their land without a fight.

Fighting Against the Calusa Indians

The Calusa Indians had lived in southwest Florida for a long time before the Spanish arrived. The Calusa were good farmers who grew corn, beans, and other crops in their gardens. And they were good fishermen and builders, too. They built **canals** (long ditches for water to flow through). They also made beautiful woodcarvings.

An artist drew this picture of a canal leading into a Calusa village.

When the Spanish arrived, the Calusa showed that they were also fierce fighters. A few months after Ponce de León came to Florida, the Calusa attacked the Spanish settlement. During the fight, a poison arrow struck Ponce de León in the leg. His leg became infected. Soon, the infection spread to the rest of his body.

Soldiers carrying Ponce de León to his ship
after he was struck by an arrow

Ponce de León needed a doctor, but the nearest doctor was on the island of Cuba, 90 miles away. The settlers decided to leave Florida and sail to Cuba.

By the time the settlers got to Cuba, it was too late to save Ponce de León. He died a few days later. He was 47 years old.

Ponce de León was buried in Cuba, and his body stayed there for almost 400 years. Then, in 1909, his body was moved to Puerto Rico, where he had lived for many years. The body was put in a tomb in San Juan Cathedral.

San Juan Cathedral

How Ponce de León's Discoveries Changed the World

Ponce de León's discoveries changed the world by getting Europeans more interested in the Americas. Ponce de León and his men were the first Europeans to see Florida, and their stories made other Europeans want to build settlements there.

When Ponce de León was wounded in 1521, the Spanish settlers left Florida with him. But 14 years later, in 1565, more Spanish settlers went back and built a town called St. Augustine. Today St. Augustine is the oldest European settlement in the United States.

The Spanish town of St. Augustine

Ponce de León's other great discovery was the Gulf Stream. This discovery helped settlers stay in touch with people in Europe because their ships could now travel faster between their new and old homes. This made more European settlers decide to move to the Americas.

The settlements in the Americas were good for the Europeans, but they were not good for the native people of the Americas. The Europeans got new land for settlements, but they took this land away from the native people. Millions of native people were killed in battle or died from diseases that the Europeans brought with them. Today we are still learning more about how these people lived. And we are still learning about what happened to them when Europeans arrived in their land.

Summary

In this article, you read about Ponce de León's second voyage to Florida. On this voyage, he went to Florida to start a Spanish settlement. But the Calusa Indians who lived in Florida attacked the settlers. Ponce de León was wounded by a poison arrow and died a few days later.

Ponce de León's discoveries changed the world by helping Europeans settle the Americas. That was a good change for Europeans, but it was a bad change for millions of Native Americans who died after the Europeans arrived.

Glossary

Word	Definition	Page
Americas	North America, South America, and the islands in the Caribbean Sea	4
canal	a long ditch for water to flow through	48
harbor	a place where ships can stay and be protected from bad weather	29
knight	a soldier who fought on horseback for the king	12
Moors	Muslims who lived in northern Africa and southern Spain	14
plantation	a large farm	27
settlement	a new place where people have come to live	21
settlers	people who go to a new place or country and build homes there	47

About the Author

Wendy Frey grew up in New York City, and went to college in Iowa. One of Wendy's first jobs was working as an editor on a radio show. Then, she decided she wanted to write books, so she went back to college to study writing. Since then, she has written history books for young people. She also writes poetry and is working on a novel.

Wendy is interested in painting, photography, sculpture, and travel. She has visited Asia, Europe, Africa, and Central America.

About the Narrator

Gary Price grew up on a big dairy farm in Iowa, with cows, horses, pigs and chickens. The farm grew enough food to feed all the animals and his family, too. Now Gary lives near Chicago. He works as an actor on the radio and on TV. He has also been a radio DJ and even had a job playing the voice of God!

A Note to the Teacher

Start-to-Finish Core Content books are designed to help students achieve success in reading to learn. From the provocative cover question to the carefully structured and considerate text, these books promote inquiry, active engagement, and understanding. Not only do students learn curriculum-relevant content, but they learn how to read with understanding. Here are some of the features that make these books such powerful aids in teaching and learning.

Structure That Supports Inquiry and Understanding

Core Content books are carefully structured to encourage students to ask questions, identify main ideas, and understand how ideas relate to one another. The structural features of the Gold Core Content books include the following:

- **"Getting Started":** A concise introduction engages students in the book's topic and explicitly states what they will learn.
- **Clearly focused articles:** Each of the following articles focuses on a single topic at a length that makes for a comfortable session of reading.
- **"Questions This Article Will Answer":** Provocative questions following the article title reflect the article's main ideas. Each question corresponds to a heading within the article.
- **Article introduction:** An engaging opening leads to a clear statement of the article topic.
- **Carefully worded headings:** The headings within each article are carefully worded to signal the main idea of the section and reflect the opening questions.
- **Clear topic statements:** Within each article section, the main idea is explicitly stated so that students can distinguish it from supporting details.
- **"Summary":** A brief Summary in each article recaptures the main ideas signaled by the opening questions, text headings, and topic statements.

Text That Is Written for Success™

Every page of a Core Content book is the product of a skilled team of educators, writers, and editors who understand your students' needs. The text features of these books include the following:

- **Mature treatment of grade level curriculum:** Core Content is age and grade-appropriate for the older student who is actively acquiring reading skills. The books also contain information that may be new to any student in the class, empowering Core Content readers to contribute interesting information to class discussions.
- **Idioms and vocabulary:** The text limits the density of new vocabulary and carefully introduces new words, new meanings of familiar words, and idioms. New subject-specific terms are bold-faced and included in the Glossary.
- **Background knowledge:** The text assumes little prior knowledge and anchors the reader using familiar examples and analogies.
- **Sentence structure:** The text uses simple sentence structures whenever possible, but where complex sentences are needed to clarify links between ideas, the structures used are those which research has shown to enhance comprehension.

For More Information

To find out more about Start-to-Finish Core Content, visit www.donjohnston.com for full product information, standards and research base.